CHRISTIAN X
AND
QUEEN ALEXANDRINE

Royal Couple
Through the World Wars

by Jens Gunni Busck

Published in cooperation with the Royal Danish Collection

CONTENTS

Plaque featuring Prince Christian and Princess Alexandrine's crowned mirror monogram and the date 1898. Produced by Royal Copenhagen on the occasion of the Couple's wedding.

Christian X c. 1920.

FOREWORD

The grandfather and grandmother of Denmark's reigning monarch HM Queen Margrethe II, King Christian X and Queen Alexandrine, were the third couple from the House of Glücksburg to ascend to the Danish throne.

The Historiographer of the Royal Orders, Professor Knud J. V. Jespersen, dr. phil, has been of invaluable help and is herewith cordially thanked. Last and not least a heartfelt thank you to Kong Christian Den Tiendes Fond for having contributed to the realization of the publication with financial support.

Birgit Jenvold
Curator

THE EQUESTRIAN KING AND THE QUEEN WHO STOOD BEHIND HIM

Christian X's study is preserved in Christian VIII's Palace at Amalienborg as though he had just left it. A royal home, too, bears witness to its resident's temperament and interests, and the King's study displays an obvious theme: an impressive arrangement of sabres, bayonets, pistols and rifles hangs on the wall, centred on a breast plate, which stands as a powerful manifestation of military spirit. Around the room stand figurines of soldiers, and in the corner by the heavy writing chair sits Ogier the Dane and almost gives the impression of being there as an adviser whose task was to whisper in the King's ear. In this room no one is left in any doubt that Christian X saw himself as the protector of the realm, and that there was a reason for his oft-cited declaration: "I am a soldier in life and soul".

Of course, Christian X did not have the opportunity to prove himself as a military commander. He ruled a realm which was drastically reduced after the defeat by Prussia and Austria in 1864, and was restricted to a neutral defence policy in relation to the surrounding great powers. Furthermore, as the constitutional king in a democratic system Christian X had only modest political powers. Nevertheless, he achieved great political significance as the Danish monarch during two world wars, and in his last years "The Equestrian King" managed to secure for himself unique popularity thanks to his role during the German Occupation. On his death in 1947 it was even decided that his coffin should be decorated with a freedom fighter's armband – not because Christian X had been directly involved in the resistance, but because during the Occupation he came to stand as a national rallying point and symbol of the Danish resistance. This gave him an unusually favourable legacy, which to a large degree has helped secure the Royal Family's continued popularity in Denmark.

At around 6'7" tall, Christian X could hardly avoid casting a shadow over his queen, but by all accounts she preferred it that way. Queen Alexandrine was a

Christian X in his study in about 1940.

musical, cultivated person who in no way sought public recognition. She was German and was therefore at the outset not a prospective queen who delighted the general populace, since the defeat to Prussia and Austria was far from forgotten when Prince Christian married her in 1898. She performed, however, her role in an exemplary manner and in her unobtrusive way also became a popular queen. Even though Queen Alexandrine appears as a slightly indistinct figure in Danish history, there is no doubt that she was of vital importance on the domestic front – both for Christian X and for their children, Prince Frederik (IX) and Prince Knud, for whose upbringing she had the main responsibility.

Prince Christian's Upbringing

Christian Carl Frederik Albert Alexander Vilhelm was born at Charlottenlund Palace on 26 September 1870 as the eldest son of Crown Prince Frederik (1843-1912) and Crown Princess Lovisa (1851-1926). The child's sex was naturally a cause of enthusiasm for the family, as it secured the line of succession for the House of Glücksburg, which had been founded seven years previously when Christian IX became King of Denmark. Over time Prince Christian became the elder brother of no fewer than seven siblings, who were born with great age differences over a twenty-year period, and he developed an especially close relationship with Prince Carl, who was two years younger than Christian and in 1905 was chosen to be King of Norway, taking the name Haakon VII.

Crown Princess Lovisa watched carefully over her children's upbringing, which was marked by strict discipline and a tight schedule with plenty of exercise and lots of homework. Prince Christian and Prince Carl were taught together in the family's two homes, Charlottenlund Palace and Brockdorff's Palace at Amalienborg (now Frederik VIII's Palace) respectively. They constituted their own little school, in which the various teachers were practically their only contacts outside the home. The princes in fact had no opportunity to associate with other playmates than one another.

As far as one can tell, Prince Christian's childhood home was not particularly harmonious. His father was weighed down by the thorough disregard he experienced in his relationship with his own father, Christian IX, who openly favoured the younger siblings. Crown Prince Frederik found himself waiting as heir ap-

parent for most of his life, while his father meticulously cut him off from any kind of influence. His mother was also far from popular within the Royal Family—in fact she was effectively frozen out—and her involvement with the Inner Mission, which increased over the years, further distanced her from her in-laws.

This situation can hardly have avoided affecting the atmosphere in the home, and with his parents in a marginalized position it is really quite understandable that Prince Christian found his most important role model outside the home, namely in the figure of the aged king, Christian IX. For Crown Prince Frederik, it must have been a conscious strategy not to pass his poor relationship with his father on to Prince Christian, for Prince Christian idolized his paternal grandfather, and in his life as king Christian X largely ruled in the style of his grandfather. He almost entirely assumed Christian IX's conservative understanding of royal power, and to an even greater extent than he built his image up around his background as an officer.

In spite of the problems which may be associated with a strict, authoritarian upbringing, it seems to have given Prince Christian some advantages later in life. It certainly made it easy for him to conduct himself in the military with its regularity and fixed routines, and a connection can be seen between the daily long walks of his childhood and the horse riding with which Christian X persisted in his adult life. The fixed framework of his upbringing was no doubt also a prerequisite for the tremendously voluminous, consistent diary keeping which Prince Christian began already as a sixteen-year-old in 1886 and continued until his death in 1947.

He also found, though, in his late teens, an important recreation at the theatre, where the prince became a frequent guest. Not least the female opera stars were the focus of his attention, and he sent fan mail and had private concerts organized.

In the spring of 1889, Prince Christian became the first Danish heir to the throne to take 'studentereksamen', the equivalent of A-levels. At this stage, too, the lessons had been taken in private, and when, after two years of preparation, he took the exam, the country's leading figures were strongly represented at the examination. In accordance with a ministerial proviso the prince was not given grades, but was judged to have "passed", and was thus ready to begin his career in earnest.

The Crown Couple Frederik (VIII) and Lovisa with their two eldest children, the princes Christian (X) and Carl (Haakon VII), 1873. At that time it was common for little boys to wear dresses.

The Military Career

On 6 May 1889, Prince Christian enlisted for service in the Royal Life Guards. As an eighteen-year-old, he had been appointed lieutenant by his royal grandfather, but he entered the Life Guards as a private. His only privilege was to live at home at Amalienborg; he otherwise shared his comrades' conditions and took pride in doing so. In spite of his relatively isolated upbringing, he felt at home amongst the guards and associated with them with a naturalness and plainness which at the time wasn't a given for an heir to the throne. The recruit training was completed after six months, after which Prince Christian embarked on the actual officer training. He passed the officer school's entry exam with fine results in the spring of 1891, and thereafter served for a time as a lieutenant with his former company in the Life Guards.

Due to his height and slender build, Prince Christian was advised not to train as an equestrian officer, but all the same he enlisted in the cavalry's second lieutenant school in Randers in November 1891. He spent six months there, gaining familiarity with horses and gaining riding abilities which would be of great use to him later in life. Thereafter he served as an officer in the 3rd dragoon regiment in Aarhus for six months, where, as in Randers, he made himself enormously popular. The sojourn in Jutland gave Prince Christian the chance to stand on his own feet for the first time, which he clearly thrived on. In the press he was called "the Jutlandic prince", and his successful conduct was an important prerequisite for the construction of Marselisborg Palace on the outskirts of Aarhus as a wedding present for the Prince and his wife around the turn of the century.

Following the Jutlandic adventure, Prince Christian returned to the Life Guards, in which he served for a number of years and was appointed captain in 1898. Hereafter he regularly held the captain's watch at Amalienborg, and his mili-

Group picture from a family gathering at Fredensborg Palace in 1883. Prince Christian is at the lower left; his grandparents are behind him. Next to Queen Louise, immediately in front of the door, stands Tsar Alexander III of Russia, who was married to Prince Christian's paternal aunt, Empress Dagmar (in front of her husband, holding the hands of the sisters Princess Alexandra and Princess Thyra).

Christian X shown in gala uniform and decorated with orders as a motif on matchboxes is presumably the most widespread royal portrait in Danish history. These "royal" matches appeared in 1904 and were produced until the King died in 1947.

tary career was crowned by an appointment as colonel and chief executive of the Life Guards in 1906, after he had become Crown Prince. At the time he was a dedicated soldier who knew his craft down to the last detail, and he served in the position of chief impeccably until his duties as Crown Prince became too extensive.

Christian X's activities as King were thus based on a long and meritorious career in the army, during which the military mores became almost part of his nature. In general, he preferred to express himself in straightforward, unaffected phrases, as one did in the army, and he was therefore not always on the same wavelength as the academically educated politicians he had to work with.

A Prince in Love

As the heir to the throne Prince Christian naturally had to consider his choice of life partner carefully. He was the object of much positive attention from the girls in Copenhagen's society life and was quite capable of socializing at balls, but with a view to marriage there were other considerations to take into account. He had to find his future wife in one of the ruling houses of Europe, which at that time were still numerous, since Prince Christian wished to continue the dynastic line which had been founded by his grandparents, who even in their own time were known as "Europe's in-laws".

The first interesting and documented event in the Prince's romantic life occurred when, he fell head over heels in love. The object of his attentions was Princess Marguerite of Orleans. She was the younger sister of the slightly eccentric Princess Marie, who in 1885 had married the youngest son of Christian IX and Queen Louise, Prince Valdemar. Princess Marguerite was staying in Copenhagen in the autumn of 1893, and during this period remarks about the Princess creep into Prince Christian's diaries more and more often. In terms of status she was also a suitable candidate for Queen, and shortly before Christmas the Prince plucked up courage and proposed, but received neither a yes nor a no. He was anguished for the entirety of the following year and in his diaries swung constantly between bright dreams for the future, hope, insecurity, and despair. He didn't receive the final rejection of his proposal until January 1895, and was heartbroken for a long time thereafter.

It is not entirely clear when Prince Christian first met Princess Alexandrine. It is possible that they had already met at the end of 1896, when he and his father passed through Schwerin after a stay in Vienna, but it wasn't until the following year that it developed into anything serious. In March 1897, Prince Christian had recovered from his heartbreak enough to travel to Cannes, which at the time was a favoured winter residence for Europe's royalty and their families. The twenty-six-year-old Prince was very conscious of the fact that it was high time he found himself a bride, and through his paternal grandmother, Queen Louise, he presumably knew all about the suitable candidates who resided in Cannes at the time.

It was hardly a coincidence, either, that his first courtesy call during his stay was to Frederick Francis III, Grand Duke of Mecklenburg-Schwerin, whose eld-

Queen Alexandrine's beautifully located childhood home, the palace in Schwerin. The large building today houses both a museum and the parliament of the German state of Mecklenburg-Vorpommern.

Cannes 26.3.98.

est daughter, at seventeen, was marriageable. The visit to the ducal home gave rise to further visits, and a couple of weeks later, on 22 March, the engagement was finalized. The proposal occurred in rather romantic circumstances on a small island off Cannes, and everything indicates that the young couple were truly in love from the outset. They later returned to the island many times during their marriage.

The Future Queen

Princess Alexandrine Auguste was born in Schwerin in northern Germany on Christmas Eve 1879. Her mother was Grand Duchess Anastasia Mikhailovna of Russia. Alexandrine was the eldest of three siblings, and the family lived a relatively withdrawn life, albeit with excellent connections. The Grand Duke had asthma, which caused the family to reside in southern latitudes for a large part of the year, first in Italy, later in Cannes. Alexandrine, or Adini as she was known, had received just as thorough a schooling as Prince Christian had in Denmark, though it was less strict. The educational standards for ducal daughters were generally very high, as the girls had to be able to enter any European court. This demanded versatility and confidence. It was taken for granted that Princess Alexandrine could speak fluent French and English as well German and Russian, which were the mother tongues of her parents. A high degree of book learning was expected, just as schooling in music was a plus, and Princess Alexandrine was fortunately endowed with a superior ear for languages and a sparkling musicality. At an early age she played the piano with great technical mastery, which was an interest she later passed on to her son Prince Frederik. Another important part of her upbringing was the many sporting activities. Rowing, tennis, golf, and sailing were some of the disciplines which were cultivated by the family, and Princess Alexandrine was heavily involved both as participant and spectator. Later on, too, as Crown Princess and Queen of Denmark, she continued to take exercise, and golf in particular was a pastime she appreciated.

Already as a young girl Princess Alexandrine had chosen "True until death" as her motto, and thus formulated an important feature of her personality. It was in her nature to keep herself in the background, but she demonstrated a thorough helpfulness and loyalty towards the people and the tasks she had taken responsibility for. Unlike her future husband, who could be a little irascible and was not always entirely considerate towards his surroundings, she was a mild and restrained person who with time developed true mastery in smoothing things over when he became too sharp.

That Prince Christian was to marry a German princess could not, of course, avoid raising critical voices, and even though the engagement was based on romantic feelings there was a widespread perception at the time that it was politically motivated. The author Henrik Pontoppidan, for example, commented ironically on it in the newspaper Politiken: "The young Princess of Mecklenburg comes to us now as a spirit of peace with a palm branch in her hand. A young robe of love is laid over the old injuries". The Princess was able, however, to overcome the enormous distrust and animosity which in the years after 1864 was directed at Germany in the minds of Danes, not least because she quickly learned Danish and moreover proved to be thoroughly loyal to her new country.

Princess Alexandrine's father died suddenly in April 1897, immediately after the engagement, and the wedding had to be postponed due to the period of mourning. The young couple, meanwhile, almost managed to kill themselves when, shortly before the wedding, they crashed in something as newfangled as an automobile in the mountains above Cannes. Fortunately they both escaped with nothing worse than some bad scratches, and the wedding could take place in Cannes on 26 April 1898 as planned.

To come to Denmark from the freer life of Schwerin and Cannes must have been an upheaval for Princess Alexandrine. Even though the Royal Family wasn't followed as intently by the press at that time as it is today, people then also wanted to know what the royalty were doing, and for a shy and reticent person it must inevitably have been stressful. There is, however, no evidence to assert anything other than that Adini's initial period in Denmark was overall idyllic. The couple resided at Sorgenfri Palace where their first child, Prince Frederik (IX), was born on 11 March 1899. Thus Denmark had three generations of heirs to the throne, and already the year after the couple had their second (and last) child, Prince Knud, who was born on 27 July 1900.

At the turn of the century the young family moved into Levetzau's Palace at Amalienborg (now Christian VIII's Palace), but they frequently returned to Sor-

The bridal couple on 26 April 1898. Here the photograph has caught them at a relaxed moment during the otherwise formal photography session.

The so-called Four Kings Picture of 1899, which became widely known, for example as a postcard. King Christian IX is holding his great-grandchild, the later Frederik IX. On the left stands the baptized child's paternal grandfather, Crown Prince Frederik (VIII), who acceded to the throne on the death of his father in 1906. To the right stands the little prince's proud father, Prince Christian.

genfri. After Marselisborg Palace was completed in 1902, the family began to stay in Aarhus when their duties allowed it. In 1914, Christian X and Queen Alexandrine had Klitgården, which would become their most cherished summer haven, built near Skagen.

The couple lived in relative seclusion in the first years, because of the children, of course, but also because the death of Queen Louise in 1898 had greatly curbed court life in general. The Queen's death, which caused Prince Christian great sorrow, had, however, heralded a generational change, and the little fam-

Prince Christian and Princess Alexandrine with their first-born child, Prince Frederik (IX), in 1899 at Christian VIII's Palace at Amalienborg, which was Christian X and Queen Alexandrine's residence in Copenhagen from about 1900 onwards. Today the Palace houses the Royal Danish Collection's department at Amalienborg, where interiors from the Crown Couple's time can still be seen.

ily suddenly had a lot more to see to following the death of Christian IX in 1906, with which Prince Christian and Princess Alexandrine became Crown Couple.

The Crown Couple

The introduction of parliamentarism in 1901 entailed reduced – and not particularly well-defined – political influence for the monarch, who had to find his own feet in the new political reality. The new king, Frederik VIII, was well-disposed towards reform and was positive about the parliamentarian principle. The same could not be said for his son, Crown Prince Christian, but the collaboration between King and Crown Prince functioned well enough in the following years, in any case better than it had in the previous generation.

A contrast between the King and his son was seen in connection with the defence question, which was one of the big topics of the time. Around the turn of the century it was clear that Denmark's defence policy would have to remain neutral, but the problem was to establish a defence which, on the one hand, was strong enough to convince Germany's opponents that Denmark couldn't simply be overrun by Germany, but on the other wouldn't be seen by Germany as an act of aggression on the part of Denmark. In 1906-07, in great secrecy, and with the consent of Frederik VIII, Prime Minister J.C. Christensen had initiated a dialogue with Germany in order to convince the Germans that Denmark would not join Germany's enemies in the event of the outbreak of war. Very few were privy to the process, and Crown Prince Christian wasn't one of them. He had a quite different, inflexible attitude towards Germany, and unwittingly behaved like a bull in a china shop when, at the 250th anniversary of the Life Guards in 1908, he expressed his unambiguous support for a strong fortification of Copenhagen against Germany. This was presumably also the reason why shortly afterwards the Crown Prince had to move with his family to Odense, where he acted as chief of the Funen brigade in the autumn.

In effect, the stay on Funen was the end of his military career, for thereafter Crown Prince Christian became more involved in his father's work. He played a major role in the governmental crisis which led to the defence settlement in 1909, which he was very dissatisfied with the result of, and which presumably

laid the foundation for his unrelenting scepticism towards politicians. Crown Prince Christian thought that the elected leaders allowed petty party political issues to weigh more heavily than patriotism, and he therefore came to see himself as the only guarantor of the safety of the realm. Conversely, there were several leading politicians who in the course of the negotiations came to view the heir to the throne with scepticism; he appeared to them to be an irascible moralizer with a deficient understanding of the political game.

Christian's time as Crown Prince was on the whole, however, a quiet time of waiting for the heirs to the throne. They lived a harmonious family life with regular stays at Marselisborg and frequent sailing trips in the coastal waters, and of course they were very much occupied with their children during these years. Christian X brought up his children with the same strictness that had characterized his own upbringing, and Prince Frederik and Prince Knud allegedly learned to have respect for the big ruler which their father kept on his desk for the purpose of punishment. Primarily, however, the children were raised by Alexandrine, whose mild character undoubtedly served as a very expedient counterbalance to her husband. As Crown Princess she had been given more official and state duties, and she placed great emphasis on being well-informed, but also reserved time to cultivate her own interests. Music was important in the home, and Alexandrine was pleased to see that Prince Frederik listened attentively. The Crown Princess also loved to use her hands, and she sewed, knitted, made lace, and not least embroidered to an advanced standard, which resulted in many truly demanding works, often for charitable causes.

With her creative abilities and her joy in family life, Alexandrine was probably quite happy with a relatively peaceful life such as theirs, while the Crown Prince, who was now forty years old, was probably subject to a certain amount of impatience. He had, however, more to see to as Frederik VIII grew more infirm, and after just six years as Crown Prince his reign was to begin.

Succession to the Throne

Frederik VIII died of a heart attack on the evening of 14 May 1912 in Hamburg on a lonely walk in the city center. From one day to the next Prince Christian had to adjust to taking office; the following morning he and his wife travelled from Sorgenfri to Lyngby Church to receive the blessing of the Church, after which, in the afternoon, Christian X was proclaimed King from the balcony of Christian VII's Palace at Amalienborg. This was an event which was a cause for celebration, not least because Frederik VIII hadn't attained great popular support as king. He had acceded to the throne at an advanced age, spoke with a German accent, and was fairly modest and civilian in behaviour, whereas the now forty-one-year-old Christian X cut a more stately figure, spoke with a Copenhagen accent, and was flanked by a still youthful queen as well as a promising thirteen-year-old Crown Prince.

Prince Frederik and his younger brother Prince Knud c. 1905. Sailor suits became popular as fashionable children's clothing amongst the European royal houses from the mid-1800s and quickly spread to other social classes. This summer "uniform" was often of white cotton with blue stripes, while the winter version was of blue wool with white ribbons.

Part of the crowd in front of Christian VII's Palace at Amalienborg on 15 May 1912, when Christian X was proclaimed King.

Christian X on summer holiday in Skagen, photographed by his wife. The King wears a black armband on his left upper arm, which dates the picture to the summer of 1912, shortly after the death of his father, Frederik VIII. Photography was one of Queen Alexandrine's creative interests, which also resulted in charity when a selection of her private photos, including this motif, was published in 1915 and was sold for the benefit of needy families.

Christian X chose the authoritative and straightforward motto "My Lord. My Country. My Honour", which was not empty rhetoric for him, since he had direct faith in God's leadership and without doubt felt a sincere responsibility for his fatherland and people. He caused great jubilation when he rounded off his short speech with the forceful words, "Denmark's fortune, freedom, and independence will be my goal, and all Danish men who share this aim – shake hands on it. May God protect and bless our old fatherland. Long live Denmark!"

The First Years as Monarch

Although the new king was the object of broad popular enthusiasm, the leading politicians soon gained a more nuanced picture of Christian X. This was due both to his opinions and to his somewhat awkward personality. From his mother Christian X had inherited a tendency towards mood swings; he could quickly oscillate between outbursts of anger and more or less obvious breakdowns. In stressful situations he tended to evade the question and change the subject. Furthermore, in general he wasn't inclined to listen to points of view which were contrary to his own conservative values, and this made it difficult for him to keep up with the rapid changes of the time, during which the working class won ever greater influence. Christian X was also under the impression that his popular support gave him a special claim to influence, which the various governments didn't always agree with.

Christian X and Queen Alexandrine, also in the summer of 1912.

With his background as a soldier Christian X took great interest in defence issues, and from the beginning of his reign there was a public expectation—particularly in conservative circles—that he would act to the benefit of the army. Funds were collected to develop the fortifications around Dyrehaven (The Deer

Park) – "close the hole in the northern front", as it was said – and the newspaper Jyllands-Posten appealed directly to the King to take initiatives on defence policy. This he of course couldn't do by direct political interference, but he applied pressure to promote the cause.

Christian X couldn't in general avoid coming into conflict with his ministers, as he wished to act independently as King and harboured a profound scepticism regarding parliamentarism. He wanted to maintain the influence to which the monarch could still lay claim, and therefore had to oppose the political climate of the time, which was moving towards returning the constitution to the provisions of the law of 1849. The conservative forces in the Landsting (a now abolished house of parliament in the earlier bicameral system) had gained decisive influence in the so-called "revised" constitution of 1866, which was still in force. Amongst other provisions, it gave the monarch the right to appoint a number of the members of the Landsting, and it underscored the king's right to appoint his ministers. When a revision of the constitution came on the agenda immediately after his accession, Christian X wasn't willing to strip the royally appointed Landsting members of their privileged position, and saw it as an unreasonable restriction of his political latitude.

The revision of the constitution was unavoidable in the long run, and although the Monarch retained the right to appoint his ministers, Christian X was far from satisfied when the law was introduced in 1915 – not least because he had profound misgivings about giving women the right to vote. When the Women's March came to Amalienborg to celebrate the 1915 constitution, the King felt it necessary to remind the deputation of the women of their domestic duties. And when the author and admiral's wife Emma Gad (known for *Takt og Tone*, her book on etiquette) declared to Christian X that it was the happiest day of her life, the King reportedly advised her to go home and make coffee for her husband.

World War I

The new constitution had been approved in a historical situation in which the question of the constitution, like so many other things, was overshadowed by the fact that Europe was in flames.

Shortly after the outbreak of the war in 1914, Christian X had had the opportunity to intervene in defence policy and go his own way, bypassing the Social Liberal government. This occurred when the Danish government in August 1914 was asked by Germany to lay a blockade of mines in the Great Belt strait, which in principle would be directed against both the war's parties, but would in reality give Germany a defence against the British navy. The Social Liberal government decided to meet the request, and to everyone's surprise the otherwise anti-German King Christian made no objections. This was, however, because he had received intelligence that the mines were not armed, and he leaked this information (which in fact was incorrect) to the British envoy in Copenhagen and to his cousin George V of the United Kingdom. This came to be of no practical

To the extent this was possible, the Royal Couple visited Cannes every summer, and Christian X's participation in a number of sailing races resulted in positive attention. Christian X was made an honorary citizen of Cannes in 1931. This bust, which can be seen in a little garden in the town, was erected in 1954.

import, but it was an involvement which, to put it politely, was at the limits of the King's authority.

During the war Christian X was constantly encouraged by conservative circles to oppose the Social Liberal government under Carl Theodor Zahle, and this happened almost of its own accord, as the King and the Prime Minister couldn't stand each other. Fundamental disagreement prevailed, and it continued to be the question of Denmark's military preparedness which gave rise to most of the tensions, since the King, on behalf of the army, opposed all reductions of the defence forces. He was also extremely displeased when Denmark sold the Danish West Indies to the USA in 1917, but it was not possible for him to prevent this.

Despite all the problems, the collaboration with the Social Liberal government was maintained, throughout the war, and that a collapse was avoided was not least due to the King's good relations with the Minister of Finance Edvard Brandes. The aged minister functioned as a bridge between the King and the Prime Minister, and for Christian X Brandes was also an important mentor in *Realpolitik*.

1920: The Easter Crisis and the Reunification

Nineteen twenty was a landmark year for Christian X personally and for the Royal Family as an institution. The government was under pressure on several fronts at the time, and the most important subject of contention was Schleswig. Following the defeat of Germany in World War I, a new border was to be drawn between Germany and Denmark, and like the Opposition the King held that the government ought to advocate a more southerly border demarcation than that which the two referendums of 10 February and 14 March had specified. A major goal in this regard was to incorporate Flensburg into Denmark despite a German majority in the city.

On 29 March 1920 the Prime Minister was received by Christian X and mentioned on the basis of this disagreement that the monarch was free to dismiss his ministers. This indeed he was according to the constitution (parliamentarianism wasn't written into it until 1953), but Zahle had hardly expected Chris-

The newspaper *Social-Demokraten* interpreted Christian X's dismissal of the prime minister as a coup d'état, and at that time the abolition of the monarchy was still part of the party programme. During the years that followed, however, a conciliatory attitude would prevail among the Social Democrats under the leadership of Thorvald Stauning.

tian X to actually act on it. Nevertheless he did and thus caused the so-called Easter Crisis. After Zahle's cabinet had resigned with immediate effect, the King formed a "non-partisan" cabinet under the barrister of the Supreme Court, Otto Liebe, while the labour movement accused the monarch of perpetrating a coup d'état and demanded that the monarchy be abolished. The collective bargaining over wage levels had just broken down, so the labour movement was already prepared to do battle, which made the situation even more tense. After much

Following the defeat of Germany in World War I, there was a possibility that the northernmost parts of the lands lost in 1864 could be handed over to Denmark again, if there was a majority in favour of this as established by an internationally controlled referendum. The area was divided into two zones, and the voting took place in February and March 1920. The northernmost zone had a Danish majority and corresponds to the current 'Sønderjylland' (Southern Jutland). Campaign poster by Thor Bøgelund 1920.

to-ing and fro-ing the King therefore decided on 4 April to replace the Liebe cabinet with a parliamentary transitional government which could function until a general election was held a month later.

Christian X's behaviour during the Easter Crisis gives the impression that he put himself in a situation the consequences of which he couldn't entirely foresee. Those around him during those few days perceived him as being rather unstable, and the King presumably had the feeling that he had gone too far. He succeeded, however, in saving the situation, which very likely could have resulted in the abolition of the monarchy if he had insisted on his constitutional powers.

Just a couple of months later, however, the King became the object of an overwhelming popular homage when the Reunification with Southern Jutland was

celebrated. Forty years previously, the famous South Jutland fortune teller Jomfru Fanny ("Miss Fanny") had related a vision in which the King of Denmark, in his prime, would ride across the border on a white horse, and it was precisely this vision which was enacted on 10 July 1920. Furthermore, Christian X demonstrated his impressive ability to improvise when he lifted a little blond girl up onto the white horse and rode with her over the border as an easily understood symbol of the Danish egregore. On this occasion Christian X was celebrated as never before, and the happy event, in combination with a number of subsequent celebrations, was perfect for suppressing the memory of the problematic chain of events a few months earlier. He kept in contact with the little girl for many years afterwards.

In connection with Reunification there were festivities in all the towns of the region. This photo shows the Royal Couple's arrival in Tønder.

1920: The Easter Crisis and the Reunification   37

The Interwar Period

After the Easter Crisis, Christian X resolved to take on a more withdrawn role. The crisis had demonstrated that parliamentarism had come to stay, so the King resigned himself to the conditions even though his principles were undoubtedly unchanged.

For the Royal Couple the interwar years were characterized by frequent travels. In 1921 Christian X and Queen Alexandrine thus visited the North Atlantic dependencies for the first time as ruling couple, which had not been possible during the war. The royal visit was the cause of great joy in Greenland and the Faroe Islands, if less so in Iceland, which had been made politically independent in 1918 but still (and until 1944) shared a monarch with Denmark in a so-called personal union. More journeys to the North Atlantic followed in subsequent years, as well as a great number of state visits and holidays, and the King indulged his passion for sailing to a greater extent. The Royal Couple could also rejoice in more modern and comfortable conveyance on their tours of the country after the new royal yacht, Dannebrog, had been named by Queen Alexandrine in 1932.

One would perhaps think that the King's conservative disposition would have made him bridle at the Social Democrats, who gained power in 1924, but the opposite happened. The leader of the worker's party, Thorvald Stauning, was, when it came down to it, not at all disposed to abolish the monarchy as his party programme stated. Christian X and Stauning – particularly from 1929 on – had an excellent relationship which lasted until Stauning's death in 1942. To be sure, it was a struggle to get through the crisis of the thirties, which brought unemployment, compulsory sales, and general poverty, making it a difficult time in which to make policies, but the King and the Prime Minister had a well-functioning partnership throughout the period. A high point in Christian X and Stauning's collaboration occurred when they neutralized the "peasant's march" of 1935 by appealing to common patriotism when they received the deputation for the 40-50,000 dissatisfied peasants assembled at Amalienborg Palace Square.

Within the family much, of course, happened in the course of the two decades between the world wars. The King and Queen lost their mothers in the 1920s. Prince Knud married his cousin Princess Caroline Mathilde and in 1935 had

After the Reunification the Royal Couple often travelled in Southern Jutland. The photograph stems from a visit to Nordborg on Als in 1932 and is one of the few pictures in which Christian X seems to be enjoying himself. According to the book Kongen og Sønderjylland ["The King and Southern Jutland"], the King had asked a local pensioner how things were going. The answer was "Jow, de geæ, men de æ få ledt pæng til tobak" ["Aye, not bad, but there's too little money for tobacco"]. The King responded by giving the man a shiny two-krone coin, which in those days could buy quite a lot of tobacco.

Queen Alexandrine
in 1926.

Christian X and
Queen Alexandrine
photographed on
their silver wedding
anniversary in 1923.
Behind them stand
their sons, Prince
Knud on the left and
Crown Prince Fred-
erik on the right.

Christian X speaking on the radio, 1933.

the Royal Couple's first grandchild, Princess Elisabeth. Crown Prince Frederik married Princess Ingrid of Sweden the same year, to the great joy of both the populace and the family – Crown Princess Ingrid became one of the few people whom Christian X always treated kindly and with consideration.

An important innovation of the period was that Christian X in the course of the 1930s began to speak regularly to the populace on the radio, and the fact that

one heard the King's voice on the radio contributed to making him more present in public life. In general, the popularity of the Royal Couple increased over the years, and when Christian X and Queen Alexandrine celebrated their Silver Jubilee in 1937 they were met by a nearly unanimous chorus of homage throughout the country.

Furthermore, Christian X paid a formal visit to the German Chancellor Adolf Hitler in 1937. The Danish government was already at that point so nervous about developments in Germany that they were worried about what sort of opinions the wilful, ageing king might air to Hitler. According to the King's report, however, their conversation merely concerned the Danish effort at the Olympic Games in Berlin the previous year.

Christian X on a visit to Berlin in 1933, when he spoke with President Hindenburg on topics including the border of 1920, which at that time had not yet been approved by Germany.

The King's daily ride through Copenhagen became a prominent national symbol after the Occupation in April 1940. However, the rides were seldom accompanied by such hectic activity as here, on 26 September 1940, the King's seventieth birthday.

The german occupation of Denmark

When Germany occupied Denmark on the morning of 9 April 1940, a meeting was hurriedly held at the palace at Amalienborg, where Christian X was quick to support the decision to stop all resistance in order to avoid a bombardment. The same day, he and Stauning released a common call to the Danish population to remain calm, and later in the day the King also released a personal message in which he recommended "proper and dignified conduct" towards the occupying power.

The Crown Couple's first child, Princess Margrethe (Denmark's current Queen) was born on 16 April 1940, exactly a week after the German invasion of Denmark. "The Sunshine Princess", as she was called, was a point of light in a dark time, and the birth increased the overwhelming popularity of the Royal Family during the Occupation. The photo shows Christian X with his grandchild in the summer of 1940.

Of course Christian X was frustrated, but he had to protest by other means than fighting, and in a sense he did so by riding. The day after the German invasion Christian X, undaunted and greatly encouraged by Princess Ingrid, resumed his daily rides from Amalienborg, and he continued to go riding until October 1942, when he injured himself badly in a fall from his horse. In the first years of the Occupation, the stubbornly riding king was a strong symbol of the nation's will to survive, and this made Christian X more loved than ever before. Christian X rode, so to speak, into the sphere of national myth, and the importance he had for the Danish populace during the Occupation meant that during the war he became a force in his own right. So strong a popular perception of royal power emerged that the King, and after his riding accident Crown Prince Frederik, became political players whom nobody could ignore, neither the government, Germany, nor the Allies.

In other ways, too, Christian X demonstrated his ability to express protest within the limits imposed by the policy of cooperation. When Germany demanded that the best Danish torpedo boats be handed over early in 1941, the King was unable to prevent the handover, but he ordered the navy to fly their flags at half-mast on setting sail – without informing Foreign Minister Scavenius, who for better or worse was the leading representative of Denmark's policy of collaboration and

Christian X and Queen Alexandrine in an everyday situation in about 1945.

The so-called royal badge was worn to express nationalistic sentiments in 1940 and during the following years. Georg Jensen Silversmiths produced more than one million copies. The idea for the badge arose before the Occupation in connection with the collection for a gift from the people on the occasion of Christian X's seventieth birthday on 26 September 1940. This exemplar in silver and enamel belonged to Frederik IX.

Christian X's burial procession on 30 April 1947. The coffin bears the armband of a freedom fighter. The King was not alone in being incorporated into the resistance movement retroactively after the war.

was enraged by the King's action. The King even aired the idea of sinking Denmark's naval vessels in order to annoy the Germans, and although this wasn't achieved on this occasion the episode served as the basis for the actual sinking of the fleet two years later, on 29 August 1943.

Neither was Christian X's popular support diminished by the so-called Telegram Crisis. On his birthday in 1942, the King sent a most concise thank you in reply to Hitler's birthday telegram, which the German chancellor took as a gross insult. For Hitler, it may have been a welcome excuse to tighten his grip and install a more Germanophile government, which was indeed the consequence.

The King naturally had to take political co-responsibility by backing the government, and he sharply criticized sabotage operations when these were on the increase in 1943. It didn't diminish the King's influence, however, that the strict German demands with regard to countermeasures forced the government to resign in August of the same year. In a country without a government, royal power was an important factor in all political players' actions and considerations during the final year of the Occupation, even though in principle the King was suspended from his position. Thus Christian X's opinion in the negotiations

about a post-war government was valued, just as Denmark's request to be included among the Allies also required his approval – by British demand.

Christian X was never able completely to recover from the riding accident of 1942, so he spent his last years in a wheelchair. Following the Liberation Christian X's health declined rapidly, and he died on 20 April 1947 after having suffered a heart attack a few weeks earlier. Queen Alexandrine was with him until the end, together with the Crown Couple and other members of the family. King Christian was interred in Roskilde Cathedral in a grand ceremony on 30 April, after the coffin had stood in the Palace Chapel at Christiansborg for a week, during which it is estimated that as many as 125,000 Danes came to take leave of him.

After Christian X's death, Alexandrine wished to continue to be called "Queen" rather than "Queen Dowager", and she diligently attended to her patronages and charity work even in her final years. The Queen also had the pleasure of her six grandchildren and kept herself very active until 1952, when she was diagnosed with volvulus for the second time. Surgery did not cure the Queen, and Alexandrine died on 28 December of the same year, four days after her 73rd birthday.

The Reign in Retrospect

Today very few young Danes have a precise idea about who Christian X was. For many older citizens, however, he remains an untouchable icon on his horse. Despite the fact that—to put it mildly—he had a rough-edged personality, Christian X succeeded in shaping his reign in such a way that it cannot be characterized as anything but a success story.

If one looks at his reign as a whole, 1920 strikes one as a watershed year. Until then Christian X, in his own view, had been a legitimate political player who could and should demand real political influence. He had to give up this approach after the Easter Crisis, but with the Reunification with Southern Jutland the same year he took on a more modern role as head of state – as a figure all Danes can rally around and feel familiar with. Whereas past kings had been actual rulers whom very few people knew, royal families have in the course of the 20th century become national icons everyone knows, and in Denmark it was Christian X who completed this transformation. He was monarch at a time

Queen Alexandrine photographs Christian X and their grandchild Princess Elisabeth. A summer's day in 1940, in the garden behind Frederik VIII's Palace at Amalienborg. In the background, on the left, the Crown Couple, Frederik and Ingrid, can be seen next to the pram.

Following spread: Queen Alexandrine and deaconesses knitting, probably in about 1950.

when the Royal Family had to relinquish its last real claim to power, but understood how to take on the role of national icon which can be said to have opened up—and to a very great extent this was made possible by the emergence of mass media.

The Occupation is probably a historic high-water mark for the popularity of the monarchy in Denmark. The national humiliation created a situation in which the King could hardly have avoided becoming popular, but Christian X acted consistently and with poise, becoming a rallying point for a frustrated populace. Like many other Danes, he was incorporated into the resistance movement only after the war—with the resistance fighter's armband that decorated his coffin—but he had taken his own resistance as far as he could.

When one tells the story of Christian X and Queen Alexandrine, the latter can hardly avoid fading into the background. The King found himself in the midst of history and was directly involved in a number of important events, while Alexandrine was a modest queen in an age when women were still expected to keep themselves in the background. Nevertheless a picture emerges in which her husband could only function so well as King because she supported him and simultaneously constituted an excellent counterbalance and partner. It is apparent from numerous testimonials that Christian X was heavily dependent on his wife. In many people's estimation she was the cleverer of the two, and she was the one who ran things in day-to-day life. It is therefore beyond doubt that Queen Alexandrine also has to be given a large part of the credit for Christian X's highly successful reign.

SUGGESTIONS FOR FURTHER READING

Anna Lerche and Marcus Mandal: *A Royal Family: The Story of Christian IX and His European Descendants,*
Lademann 2003.
Illustrated book about the House of Glücksburg with a foreword by Her Majesty Queen Margrethe II. Also produced as a TV documentary series for DR.

Knud J.V. Jespersen : *Rytterkongen – Et portræt af Christian 10.,*
Gyldendal 2007.
The authoritative biography of Christian X, which in contrast to older portraits is based on the main character's own diaries.

Claus Bjørn: *Blot til Pynt. Monarkiet i Danmark – i går, i dag og i morgen,*
Fremad 2001.
An insightful book about the constitutional monarchy in Denmark, with lengthy sections about each of the Danish kings since the absolute monarchy.

Randi Buchwaldt: *Kongehusets farmor og oldemor Dronning Alexandrine,*
Hernov 1998.
A little book about Queen Alexandrine, published on the occasion of the 100th anniversary of Alexandrine's arrival in Denmark on 26 May 1898.

www.kongernessamling.dk.

Christian X and Queen Alexandrine
Royal Couple Through the World Wars

Copyright © 2016
The Royal Danish Collection and Historika / Gads Forlag A/S

ISBN: 978-87-93229-44-0
Second edition, first print run

Printed in Lithuania

Text: Jens Gunni Busck
Edited by Axel Harms
Translated from Danish by Christopher Sand-Iversen
Cover and graphic design Lene Nørgaard, Propel
Printed by Clemenstrykkeriet, Lithuania

Illustrations:
Front page, p. 4, 6, 9, 10, (photo: Peter Elfelt), 12, 15, 16, 20, 21 (Photo: Carl Sonne), 22 (photo: Peter Elfelt), 24 (photo: Peter Elfelt), 26-27 (photo: Peter Elfelt), 28, 29, 30, 33, 36 (photo: Peter Elfelt), 37, 42 (photo: Peter Elfelt), 43, 44 (photo: Peter Elfelt), 45, 46 (photo: Inga Aistrup), 47 (photo: Inga Aistrup), 48 (photo: Vittus Nielsen), 49, 50, 51, 52 (photo: Inga Aistrup), 54-55, 57: The Royal Danish Collection, p. 3,13: Iben Bølling Kaufmann, p. 19: Det Kongelige Bibliotek, p. 34: Arbejderbevægelsens Bibliotek og Arkiv, p. 35: Museum Sønderjylland – Sønderborg Slot, p. 39: Kongelig Dansk Yachtklub, p. 40-41: Nordborg Lokalhistoriske Arkiv.